TABLE OF CONTENT

1.CLASSIC STRAWBERRY JAM

Prep Time: 15 mins

Cook Time: 25 mins

Total Time: 40 mins

Servings: 4 cups of

Ingredients:

- 2 lbs (about 4 cups of) fresh strawberries, hulled and halved
- 2 cups of granulated sugar
- 2 tbsp lemon juice

Instructions:

1. Use a potato masher to gently mash the strawberries in a Big saucepan.
2. Add lemon juice and sugar and stir.
3. Over medium-high heat, bring to a boil, stirring often.
4. Simmer for 20 to 25 mins, or up to thickened, after lowering the heat to medium.
5. Put a little scoop on a cold plate to test it; if it wrinkles when pressed, it's done.
6. Fill sterile jars, cover, and store in the refrigerator for up to three weeks.

Nutrition (per tbsp):

Cals: 35, Carbs: 9g

Sugar: 8g, Fat: 0g

Protein: 0g

2. BLUEBERRY LEMON JAM

Prep Time: 10 mins

Cook Time: 30 mins

Total Time: 40 mins

Servings: 4 cups of

Ingredients:

- 4 cups of fresh blueberries

- 2 cups of granulated sugar
- 1 tbsp lemon zest
- 2 tbsp lemon juice

Instructions:

1. Put the blueberries, sugar, lemon juice, and zest in a saucepan.
2. Bring to a boil, then simmer up to thick, 25 to 30 mins.
3. If you want a smoother texture, mash with a potato masher.
4. Use a cold platter to check for doneness.
5. Transfer to jars, let cool fully, and then store in the refrigerator.

Nutrition (per tbsp):

Cals: 36, Carbs: 9g, Sugar: 8g

Fat: 0g, Protein: 0g

3. SPICED PEVERY JAM

Prep Time: 20 mins

Cook Time: 30 mins

Total Time: 50 mins

Servings: 5 cups of

Ingredients:

- 4 cups of peel off, chop-up ripe peveryes
- 2 cups of granulated sugar
- 2 tbsp lemon juice
- 1 tsp ground cinnamon
- 1/4 tsp ground nutmeg

Instructions:

1. Put the peveryes, sugar, lemon juice, and spices in a big saucepan.
2. Place over medium-high heat and bring to a boil.
3. Simmer for 25 to 30 mins over low heat, stirring frequently.
4. For the required consistency, mash or use a hand blender.
5. Transfer to jars and allow to cool. For long-term storage, keep in a container or the refrigerator.

Nutrition (per tbsp):

Cals: 38, Carbs: 10g

Sugar: 9g, Fat: 0g

Protein: 0g

4. BLACKBERRY VANILLA JAM

Prep Time: 15 mins

Cook Time: 25 mins

Total Time: 40 mins

Servings: 4 cups of

Ingredients:

- 4 cups of fresh blackberries
- 2 cups of sugar
- 1 tbsp lemon juice
- 1 tsp vanilla extract

Instructions:

1. In a saucepan, combine lemon juice, sugar, and blackberries.
2. After bringing to a boil, reduce the heat and simmer for 20 to 25 mins, stirring often.
3. When cooking is almost done, add vanilla extract.
4. Use a cold plate to test consistency.
5. Pour into jars and allow to cool. Keep chilled.

Nutrition (per tbsp):

Cals: 37, Carbs: 9g

Sugar: 8g, Fat: 0g

Protein: 0g

5. RASPBERRY RHUBARB JAM

Prep Time: 15 mins

Cook Time: 30 mins

Total Time: 45 mins

Servings: 5 cups of

Ingredients:

- 2 cups of chop-up rhubarb
- 2 cups of raspberries
- 2 1/2 cups of sugar
- 2 tbsp lemon juice

Instructions:

1. Put the sugar and rhubarb in a saucepan. Give it ten mins to sit.
2. Pour in the lemon juice and raspberries.
3. Bring to a boil and simmer, stirring often, for 25 to 30 mins.
4. Check the thickness with a cold plate.
5. Cool, transfer to jars, and place in the refrigerator.

Nutrition (per tbsp):

Cals: 34, Carbs: 9g

Sugar: 8g, Fat: 0g

Protein: 0g

6.APRICOT HONEY JAM

Prep Time: 15 mins

Cook Time: 25 mins

Total Time: 40 mins

Servings: 3 cups of

Ingredients:

- 2 lbs fresh apricots, pitted and chop-up
- 1 cup of honey
- 1 tbsp lemon juice
- 1/4 tsp ground ginger (non-compulsory)

Instructions:

1. Put the ginger, lemon juice, honey, and apricots in a big pot.
2. Cook over medium heat for about 15 mins, stirring often, up to the apricots are broken down.
3. To get the texture you want, use an immersion blender.
4. Cook for ten more mins or up to thickened.
5. Leave 1/4-inch headroom when pouring into sterilized jars. Cool after sealing.
6. For shelf stability, process in a water bath or keep in the refrigerator for up to a month.

Nutrition (per tbsp):

Cals: 35, Carbs: 9g

Sugars: 8g, Fiber: 0.3g

Protein: 0.1g

7. FIG AND ORANGE JAM

Prep Time: 20 mins

Cook Time: 30 mins

Total Time: 50 mins

Servings: 3 cups of

Ingredients:

- 2 lbs fresh figs, stems take outd and chop-up
- 1/2 cup of orange juice
- 2 tsp orange zest
- 1 1/2 cups of sugar
- 1 tbsp lemon juice

Instructions:

1. In a saucepan, combine the figs, lemon juice, sugar, orange juice, and zest.
2. Bring to a simmer and cook up to the figs are soft, stirring often.
3. Blend or mash as you like.
4. Simmer up to thick, 10 to 15 more mins.
5. Seal after transferring to sterile jars. Before storage, let it cool fully.

Nutrition (per tbsp):

Cals: 40, Carbs: 10g

Sugars: 9g, Fiber: 0.4g

Protein: 0.2g

8. CHERRY ALMOND JAM

Prep Time: 25 mins

Cook Time: 35 mins

Total Time: 1 hr

Servings: 3.5 cups of

Ingredients:

- 2 lbs fresh cherries, pitted
- 1 3/4 cups of sugar
- 2 tbsp lemon juice
- 1/2 tsp almond extract

Instructions:

1. Put the lemon juice, sugar, and cherries in a big saucepan.
2. Reduce to a simmer after bringing to a boil. Stir often.
3. Cook up to thick, 30 to 35 mins.
4. Finally, stir in almond extract.
5. Seal after spooning into sterile jars.

Nutrition (per tbsp):

Cals: 42, Carbs: 11g

Sugars: 10g, Fiber: 0.3g

Protein: 0.1g

9. PLUM CINNAMON JAM

Prep Time: 20 mins

Cook Time: 30 mins

Total Time: 50 mins

Servings: 3 cups of

Ingredients:

- 2 lbs ripe plums, pitted and chop-up
- 1 1/2 cups of sugar
- 1 tbsp lemon juice
- 1/2 tsp ground cinnamon

Instructions:

1. In a saucepan, combine all ingredients over medium heat.
2. Bring to a boil, then simmer for 25 to 30 mins, stirring.
3. If you want a smoother texture, blend.
4. Keep cooking up to the consistency of jam is achieved.
5. Fill sterile jars, then cover.

Nutrition (per tbsp):

Cals: 38, Carbs: 9g

Sugars: 8g, Fiber: 0.4g

Protein: 0.1g

10. TRIPLE BERRY JAM

Prep Time: 15 mins

Cook Time: 25 mins

Total Time: 40 mins

Servings: 3 cups of

Ingredients:

1 cup of strawberries, hulled and chop-up

1 cup of raspberries

1 cup of blueberries

2 cups of sugar

2 tbsp lemon juice

Instructions:

1. In a saucepan, combine the lemon juice, sugar, and berries.
2. Bring over medium-high heat to a moderate boil.
3. As the berries soften, mash them and stir regularly.
4. Simmer up to thickened, 20 to 25 mins.
5. Transfer to sterile jars, cover, and allow to cool.

Nutrition (per tbsp):

Cals: 37, Carbs: 9g

Sugars: 8g, Fiber: 0.4g

Protein: 0.1g

11.APPLE JELLY WITH MINT

Prep Time: 20 mins

Cook Time: 1 hr

Total Time: 1 hr 20 mins

Servings: Makes about 5 half-pint jars

Ingredients:

- 4 lbs tart apples (such as Granny Smith), chop-up
- 6 cups of water
- 3 tbsp lemon juice
- 1 package (1.75 oz) powdered fruit pectin
- 4 cups of granulated sugar
- 1/4 cup of fresh mint leaves, lightly chop-up

Instructions:

1. Put water and apples in a big saucepan. Reduce heat, bring to a boil, and simmer for 40 mins.
2. For transparent jelly, let the juice drip overnight after straining it through cheesecloth or a jelly bag without pressing.
3. In a big saucepan, measure out 4 cups of juice. Pour in the pectin and lemon juice. Heat up to a rolling boil occurs.

4. Bring back to a boil after adding the sugar all at once. Boil vigorously for one min while stirring continuously.
5. Take off the heat and combine in the mint. foam on the surface.
6. Fill sterilized jars with heated jelly, allowing a 1/4-inch headspace. Seal after wiping the rims.
7. For five mins, process in a hot water bath.

Nutrition (Per Tbsp):

Cals: 45, Carbs: 12g

Sugar: 11g, Fat: 0g

Protein: 0g, Fiber: 0g

12. GRAPE JELLY

Prep Time: 15 mins

Cook Time: 30 mins

Total Time: 45 mins

Servings: Makes about 6 half-pint jars

Ingredients:

- 3 lbs Concord grapes, stemmed
- 1/2 cup of water
- 1 box (1.75 oz) powdered pectin
- 5 1/2 cups of granulated sugar

Instructions:

1. In a Big saucepan, combine water and crushed grapes; bring to a boil.
2. Simmer for ten mins. For clear juice, strain through a jelly bag.
3. Fill a saucepan with 4 cups of juice. Bring to a complete boil after adding the pectin.
4. Return to a vigorous boil for one min after adding the sugar.
5. Take off the heat and skim the froth.
6. Leave a 1/4-inch headroom when pouring into sterilized jars. For five mins, seal and process in a hot water bath.

Nutrition (Per Tbsp):

Cals: 50, Carbs: 13g

Sugar: 12g, Fat: 0g

Protein: 0g, Fiber: 0g

13 ELDERBERRY JELLY

Prep Time: 20 mins

Cook Time: 40 mins

Total Time: 1 hr

Servings: Makes about 5 half-pint jars

Ingredients:

- 3 lbs elderberries, stems take outd
- 1/2 cup of water
- 1 box (1.75 oz) powdered pectin
- 4 1/2 cups of granulated sugar
- 2 tbsp lemon juice

Instructions:

1. For fifteen mins, simmer elderberries with water. While cooking, crush the berries.
2. Via a jelly bag, strain. Measure out three cups of juice.
3. Fill a saucepan with juice, lemon juice, and pectin. Bring to a boil.
4. Add sugar and bring to a high boil for one min.
5. Ladle into jars after skimming the froth, leaving a 1/4-inch headspace.
6. For five mins, seal and process in a hot water bath.

Nutrition (Per Tbsp):

Cals: 48, Carbs: 12g

Sugar: 11g, Fat: 0g

Protein: 0g, Fiber: 0g

14. ROSEHIP JELLY

Prep Time: 25 mins

Cook Time: 45 mins

Total Time: 1 hr 10 mins

Servings: Makes about 4 half-pint jars

Ingredients:

- 4 cups of fresh rosehips, cleaned and trimmed
- 4 cups of water
- 1/4 cup of lemon juice
- 1 package (1.75 oz) powdered pectin
- 4 cups of sugar

Instructions:

1. Mash the rosehips to unleash their flavor after 30 mins of simmering them in water.
2. To extract juice, strain through cheesecloth overnight.
3. Add the pectin and lemon juice to three cups of measured juice. Bring to a boil.
4. Boil hard for one min after adding the sugar.
5. Pour into jars, allowing 1/4 inch headspace, after skimming the froth.
6. After sealing, cook for five mins in a boiling water bath.

Nutrition (Per Tbsp):

Cals: 45, Carbs: 11g

Sugar: 10g, Fat: 0g

Protein: 0g, Fiber: 0g

15. HOT PEPPER JELLY

Prep Time: 15 mins

Cook Time: 25 mins

Total Time: 40 mins

Servings: Makes about 5 half-pint jars

Ingredients:

- 3/4 cup of lightly chop-up green bell pepper
- 3/4 cup of lightly chop-up red bell pepper

- 1/4 cup of lightly chop-up jalapeños (seeds take outd for less heat)
- 1 1/2 cups of apple cider vinegar
- 1 box (1.75 oz) powdered pectin
- 5 cups of sugar

Instructions:

1. In a Big saucepan, combine the vinegar and peppers. Bring to a boil after adding the pectin.
2. Add the sugar all at once. Boil for one min after returning to a rolling boil.
3. Take off the heat and skim the froth.
4. Leave a 1/4-inch headroom when pouring into sterilized jars.
5. For ten mins, seal and process in a hot water bath.

Nutrition (Per Tbsp):

Cals: 52, Carbs: 13g, Sugar: 12g

Fat: 0g, Protein: 0g

Fiber: 0g

16.SLOW-COOKED APPLE BUTTER

Prep Time: 20 mins

Cook Time: 10 hrs

Total Time: 10 hrs 20 mins

Servings: 6 cups of

Ingredients

- 6 lbs apples (peel off, cored, and split)
- 2 cups of granulated sugar
- 1 cup of brown sugar
- 1 tbsp ground cinnamon
- 1/2 tsp ground cloves
- 1/4 tsp salt
- 1 tbsp vanilla extract

Instructions

1. Simmer the apples in a slow cooker. Add salt, cloves, cinnamon, and sweeteners.

2. Cook, covered, on low, stirring periodically, for 10 hrs.
3. Take out the lid and combine in the vanilla extract.
4. For a smoother texture, use an immersion blender (non-compulsory).
5. Cool and store in the freezer or refrigerator in airtight containers.

Nutrition (per 2 tbsp)

Cals: 70, Carbs: 18g

Sugars: 16g, Fiber: 1g

Fat: 0g, Protein: 0g

17. PEAR VANILLA BUTTER

Prep Time: 15 mins

Cook Time: 1 hr 30 mins

Total Time: 1 hr 45 mins

Servings: 4 cups of

Ingredients

- 5 lbs ripe pears (peel off, cored, chop-up)
- 1 cup of sugar
- 1 vanilla bean (split and scraped) or 1 tbsp vanilla extract
- 1/4 cup of lemon juice
- 1/4 tsp ground nutmeg

Instructions

1. In a Big saucepan, combine pears, sugar, lemon juice, vanilla, and nutmeg.
2. Cook for 30 mins over medium heat, or up to pears are tender.
3. Use a blender or immersion blender to puree.
4. Put back in the saucepan and simmer for approximately an hr, stirring often, over low heat, up to thickened.
5. Refrigerate or store in sterile jars.

Nutrition (per 2 tbsp)

Cals: 55, Carbs: 14g

Sugars: 12g, Fiber: 1g

Fat: 0g

Protein: 0g

18. PUMPKIN SPICE BUTTER

Prep Time: 10 mins

Cook Time: 25 mins

Total Time: 35 mins

Servings: 3 cups of

Ingredients

- 1 (29 oz) can pumpkin puree
- 1 cup of apple juice or cider
- 3/4 cup of sugar
- 1/2 cup of brown sugar
- 1 tbsp lemon juice
- 1 tbsp ground cinnamon
- 1/4 tsp ground nutmeg
- 1/4 tsp ground cloves
- 1/4 tsp salt

Instructions

1. In a saucepan, combine all the ingredients.
2. Bring to a slow boil, lower the heat, and simmer, uncovered, stirring often, up to the Mixture thickens, 25 to 30 mins.
3. Allow to cool and refrigerate in jars.

Nutrition (per 2 tbsp)

Cals: 45, Carbs: 11g

Sugars: 8g, Fiber: 1g

Fat: 0g, Protein: 0g

19. MANGO GINGER CONSERVE

Prep Time: 20 mins

Cook Time: 45 mins

Total Time: 1 hr 5 mins

Servings: 5 cups of

Ingredients

- 4 cups of chop-up ripe mango
- 1/2 cup of chop-up crystallized ginger
- 1/4 cup of lemon juice
- 1 tbsp lemon zest
- 2 cups of sugar
- 1/2 tsp ground cardamom (non-compulsory)

Instructions

1. In a saucepan, combine the mango, sugar, ginger, lemon juice, and zest.
2. Cook for 35 to 45 mins over medium heat, stirring often, up to thick and jam-like.
3. Stir in cardamom and turn off the heat.
4. Before storage, pour into sterile jars and allow to cool.

Nutrition (per 2 tbsp)

Cals: 60, Carbs: 15g, Sugars: 13g

Fiber: 0.5g, Fat: 0g

Protein: 0g

20. CRANBERRY ORANGE CONSERVE

Prep Time: 15 mins

Cook Time: 30 mins

Total Time: 45 mins

Servings: 4 cups of

Ingredients

- 3 cups of fresh cranberries
- 1 orange (zested and juiced)
- 1/2 cup of orange juice (additional)
- 1/2 cup of chop-up walnuts (non-compulsory)

- 1 apple, peel off and diced
- 1 1/2 cups of sugar
- 1/2 tsp cinnamon

Instructions

1. In a saucepan, combine the cranberries, apple, sugar, orange juice, and orange zest.
2. Bring to a boil, then lower the heat and simmer, stirring often, for 25 to 30 mins.
3. Add walnuts (if used) and cinnamon and stir.
4. Chill and refrigerate in jars.

Nutrition (per 2 tbsp)

Cals: 65, Carbs: 17g

Sugars: 14g, Fiber: 1g

Fat: 1g, Protein: 0g

21.CLASSIC DILL PICKLES

Prep Time: 20 mins

Cook Time: 10 mins

Total Time: 30 mins + 24 hrs for pickling

Servings: 4 pint jars

Ingredients:

- 2 lbs pickling cucumbers, split or whole
- 2 cups of water
- 2 cups of white vinegar
- 2 tbsp pickling salt
- 4 cloves garlic, peel off
- 4 tsp dill seeds or fresh dill sprigs
- 1 tsp black peppercorns
- Non-compulsory: 1/2 tsp crushed red pepper flakes (per jar for spice)

Instructions:

1. Clean cucumbers and slice off the ends. Tightly pack in sterile jars.

2. Fill every jar with one clove of garlic, one tsp of dill seed, peppercorns, and red pepper, if using.
3. Heat the salt, vinegar, and water in a saucepan up to they boil. To dissolve the salt, stir.
4. Cover cucumbers with hot brine, allowing a 1/2" headspace. Jars Must be sealed.
5. For shelf stability, either refrigerate or treat in a hot water bath for ten mins.
6. Before eating, let it rest for a full day, preferably a week.

Nutrition (per serving/jar):

Cals: 25 | Carbs: 5g | Protein: 1g | Fat: 0g | Sodium: 750mg

22.BREAD AND BUTTER PICKLES

Prep Time: 20 mins

Cook Time: 15 mins

Total Time: 35 mins + 24 hrs for pickling

Servings: 4 pint jars

Ingredients:

- 2 lbs cucumbers, thinly split
- 1 medium onion, thinly split
- 1/4 cup of kosher salt
- 2 cups of apple cider vinegar
- 1 cup of white vinegar
- 1 1/2 cups of sugar
- 1 tbsp mustard seeds
- 1/2 tsp celery seed
- 1/2 tsp turmeric

Instructions:

1. In a bowl, combine the cucumbers, onion, and salt. Rinse and drain after covering and chilling for one to two hrs.
2. Heat the vinegars, sugar, and spices in a pot up to they boil.
3. Bring back to a boil after adding the drained cucumber Mixture.
4. Leave 1/2" headroom when packing the heated Mixture into jars. Seal.
5. Let it remain in the refrigerator for a whole day or run it through a water bath for ten mins.

Nutrition (per serving/jar):

Cals: 100 | Carbs: 22g | Protein: 1g | Fat: 0g | Sodium: 500mg

23.PICKLED RED ONIONS

Prep Time: 10 mins

Cook Time: 5 mins

Total Time: 15 mins + 1 hr rest

Servings: 2 cups of

Ingredients:

- 1 Big red onion, thinly split
- 1/2 cup of apple cider vinegar
- 1/2 cup of water
- 1 tbsp sugar
- 1 1/2 tsp kosher salt
- Non-compulsory: 1/2 tsp black peppercorns or red chili flakes

Instructions:

1. Put the slice onions in a jar that can withstand heat.
2. Put the vinegar, water, sugar, salt, and spices in a pot. Bring to a boil.
3. Cover onions with heated liquid. Cool, then store in the refrigerator.
4. You can eat it in an hr, but it's finest 24 hrs later.

Nutrition (per 2 tbsp serving):

Cals: 10 | Carbs: 2g | Protein: 0g | Fat: 0g | Sodium: 120mg

24.SWEET PICKLED BEETS

Prep Time: 15 mins

Cook Time: 45 mins

Total Time: 1 hr + cooling

Servings: 4 pint jars

Ingredients:

- 2 lbs beets, trimmed and scrubbed
- 2 cups of sugar
- 2 cups of apple cider vinegar
- 1 cup of water
- 1/2 tsp ground cloves
- 1/2 tsp ground allspice
- 1/2 tsp cinnamon

Instructions:

1. Beets can be roasted or boiled for 40 to 45 mins to make them soft. Slice and peel.
2. Heat the water, vinegar, sugar, and spices in a pot up to they boil.
3. Simmer for 5 mins after adding the beets.
4. Fill jars, pour boiling liquid over them, and then seal.
5. Put in the refrigerator or a water bath container for half an hr.

Nutrition (per serving/jar):

Cals: 120 | Carbs: 30g | Protein: 1g | Fat: 0g | Sodium: 90mg

25.SPICY GARLIC DILLS

Prep Time: 25 mins

Cook Time: 10 mins

Total Time: 35 mins + 48 hrs to pickle

Servings: 4 pint jars

Ingredients:

- 2 lbs cucumbers
- 8 garlic cloves, smashed
- 4 tsp dill seeds
- 2 tsp red pepper flakes
- 1 tsp black peppercorns
- 2 cups of water
- 2 cups of white vinegar
- 2 tbsp pickling salt

Instructions:

1. Add two garlic cloves, one tsp dill seed, half a tsp red pepper, and a few peppercorns to every jar containing cucumbers.
2. Bring salt, vinegar, and water to a boil. Allow 1/2" headroom when pouring into jars.
3. Can in boiling water for 10 mins or seal and place in the refrigerator.
4. For maximum taste, let it rest for at least 48 hrs.

Nutrition (per serving/jar):

Cals: 20 | Carbs: 4g | Protein: 1g | Fat: 0g | Sodium: 700mg

26.PICKLED CARROTS WITH GINGER

Prep Time: 15 mins

Cook Time: 5 mins

Total Time: 20 mins (+24 hrs for pickling)

Servings: 4 cups of

Ingredients:

- 4 Big carrots, julienned or split into matchsticks
- 1 tbsp fresh ginger, peel off and thinly split
- 1 cup of white vinegar
- 1 cup of water
- 2 tbsp sugar
- 1 tbsp salt
- 1 garlic clove, smashed
- ½ tsp whole black peppercorns

Instructions:

1. Sterilize two 1-pint jars or a 1-quart jar.
2. Tightly pack the ginger and carrots inside the jar or jars.
3. Add the vinegar, water, sugar, salt, peppercorns, and garlic to a saucepan. After bringing to a boil, turn off the heat.
4. Leave ½ inch of headroom when you pour the boiling brine over the carrots.
5. After sealing the jar or jars, allow them to cool to room temperature.
6. Before serving, let it sit in the refrigerator for at least 24 hrs.

Nutrition (per 1/4 cup of):

Cals: 25, Carbs: 6g

Sugar: 4g, Sodium: 180mg

Fat: 0g, Fiber: 1g

Protein: 0g

27. PICKLED JALAPEÑO SLICES

Prep Time: 10 mins

Cook Time: 5 mins

Total Time: 15 mins (+24 hrs for pickling)

Servings: 2 cups of

Ingredients:

- 10–12 jalapeños, thinly split
- 1 cup of white vinegar
- 1 cup of water
- 2 tbsp sugar
- 1 tbsp salt
- 1 garlic clove, smashed
- ½ tsp oregano (non-compulsory)

Instructions:

1. Put the slices of jalapeño in a sanitized glass jar.
2. Add the vinegar, water, sugar, salt, oregano, and garlic to a saucepan. Bring to a boil.
3. Cover the jalapeños with the spicy brine up to they are completely immersed.
4. After allowing it to revery room temperature, cover and store in the refrigerator.
5. Before using, let it cool for at least 24 hrs.

Nutrition (per 1/4 cup of):

Cals: 15, Carbs: 3g

Sugar: 2g, Sodium: 170mg

Fat: 0g, Fiber: 1g

Protein: 0g

28. ZUCCHINI RELISH

Prep Time: 30 mins

Cook Time: 30 mins

Total Time: 1 hr (+12 hrs to salt veggies)

Servings: 4 pints

Ingredients:

- 4 cups of zucchini, lightly chop-up
- 2 cups of onion, lightly chop-up
- 1 cup of red bell pepper, lightly chop-up
- 1 cup of green bell pepper, lightly chop-up
- ¼ cup of salt
- 2½ cups of sugar
- 1 tbsp mustard seeds
- 1½ tsp celery seed
- 1½ cups of white vinegar

Instructions:

1. Combine the peppers, zucchini, and onion in a Big bowl and season with salt. Cover and leave overnight.
2. Drain and rinse veggies well.
3. Put the mustard seed, celery seed, vinegar, and sugar in a big saucepan. Bring to a boil.
4. Simmer for 30 mins after adding the veggies.
5. Fill sterilized jars with hot relish. Refrigerate or seal and process in a hot water bath for ten mins.

Nutrition (per 2 tbsp):

Cals: 35, Carbs: 9g

Sugar: 7g, Sodium: 160mg

Fat: 0g, Fiber: 0.5g

Protein: 0g

29. CORN RELISH

Prep Time: 25 mins

Cook Time: 30 mins

Total Time: 55 mins

Servings: 6 cups of

Ingredients:

- 4 cups of corn kernels (fresh or refrigerate)
- 1½ cups of red bell pepper, chop-up
- 1 cup of green bell pepper, chop-up
- 1 cup of celery, chop-up
- ¾ cup of onion, chop-up
- 1½ cups of white vinegar
- ¾ cup of sugar
- 2 tsp mustard seeds
- 1 tsp turmeric
- 1 tsp celery seed
- 1 tsp salt

Instructions:

1. Put all the ingredients in a big saucepan. Combine by stirring.
2. After bringing to a boil, lower the heat, and simmer for half an hr, stirring now and again.
3. Fill sterilized jars with hot relish, allowing ½ inch headspace.
4. Refrigerate for instant use, or seal and water bathe for 10 mins.

Nutrition (per 2 tbsp):

Cals: 40, Carbs: 10g

Sugar: 7g, Sodium: 140mg

Fat: 0g, Fiber: 1g

Protein: 1g

30. GREEN TOMATO RELISH

Prep Time: 30 mins

Cook Time: 45 mins

Total Time: 1 hr 15 mins

Servings: 5 cups of

Ingredients:

- 5 cups of green tomatoes, chop-up
- 1½ cups of onion, chop-up
- 1 cup of red bell pepper, chop-up
- 1 cup of green bell pepper, chop-up
- 1 cup of apple cider vinegar
- ¾ cup of brown sugar
- 1 tbsp salt
- 1 tsp mustard seeds
- ½ tsp ground cloves
- ½ tsp cinnamon

Instructions:

1. In a big saucepan, combine all ingredients. Bring to a boil.
2. Simmer for 45 mins over low heat, stirring often.
3. Leave ½ inch of headroom when pouring into sterile jars.
4. Process in a water bath canner for 10 mins or seal and chill.

Nutrition (per 2 tbsp):

Cals: 30, Carbs: 7g

Sugar: 5g, Sodium: 150mg

Fat: 0g, Fiber: 1g

Protein: 0g

31.APPLE CRANBERRY CHUTNEY

Prep Time: 15 mins

Cook Time: 35 mins

Total Time: 50 mins

Servings: 2 cups of

Ingredients:

- 2 medium apples, peel off, cored, and chop-up
- 1 cup of fresh or refrigerate cranberries
- ½ cup of brown sugar
- ½ cup of apple cider vinegar
- 1 mini onion, lightly chop-up
- 1 tbsp finely grated fresh ginger
- ¼ tsp ground cinnamon
- ¼ tsp ground cloves
- ⅛ tsp cayenne pepper (non-compulsory)
- Pinch of salt

Instructions:

1. Put all the ingredients in a saucepan.
2. Over medium heat, bring to a boil, stirring often.
3. Simmer uncovered over low heat for 30 to 35 mins, stirring regularly, up to the Mixture thickens and the cranberries pop.
4. After cooling, transfer to a jar or other container.
5. Use within two weeks after putting in the fridge.

Nutrition (per 2 tbsp):

Cals: 40, Carbs: 10g

Sugars: 8g, Fiber: 1g

Fat: 0g, Protein: 0g

32.TOMATO DATE CHUTNEY

Prep Time: 10 mins

Cook Time: 40 mins

Total Time: 50 mins

Servings: 2 cups of

Ingredients:

- 4 medium ripe tomatoes, chop-up
- ½ cup of chop-up dates
- ½ cup of red onion, lightly chop-up
- ½ cup of apple cider vinegar

- ¼ cup of brown sugar
- 1 tsp mustard seeds
- 1 tsp finely grated fresh ginger
- ½ tsp chili flakes
- Salt as needed

Instructions:

1. Toast the mustard seeds in a saucepan over high heat for one min.
2. Stir well after adding all other ingredients.
3. Reduce to a simmer after bringing to a boil.
4. Cook up to thickened, stirring regularly, for 35 to 40 mins.
5. Cool and keep in the refrigerator for up to two weeks in a clean container.

Nutrition (per 2 tbsp):

Cals: 45, Carbs: 11g

Sugars: 8g, Fiber: 1g

Fat: 0g

Protein: 0.5g

33.MANGO LIME CHUTNEY

Prep Time: 15 mins

Cook Time: 30 mins

Total Time: 45 mins

Servings: 2.5 cups of

Ingredients:

- 2 ripe mangoes, peel off and diced
- Zest and juice of 1 lime
- ½ cup of sugar
- ½ cup of white vinegar
- ¼ cup of golden raisins
- 1 mini red chili, chop-up
- 1 tsp finely grated ginger
- ½ tsp cumin seeds

- ¼ tsp turmeric
- Salt as needed

Instructions:

1. In a dry pan, toast cumin seeds for 30 seconds.
2. Bring to a boil after adding all the ingredients.
3. Reduce the heat and simmer up to the Mixture thickens, stirring regularly, for 25 to 30 mins.
4. After cooling, store in sterile jars. Refrigerated for three weeks.

Nutrition (per 2 tbsp):

Cals: 55, Carbs: 14g

Sugars: 10g, Fiber: 0.5g

Fat: 0g, Protein: 0g

34.SPICY PLUM CHUTNEY

Prep Time: 10 mins

Cook Time: 45 mins

Total Time: 55 mins

Servings: 2 cups of

Ingredients:

- 2 cups of plums, pitted and chop-up
- ½ cup of red onion, lightly chop-up
- ½ cup of brown sugar
- ⅓ cup of red wine vinegar
- 1 mini chili pepper, lightly chop-up
- 1 tsp finely grated fresh ginger
- ¼ tsp cinnamon
- ¼ tsp allspice
- Salt as needed

Instructions:

1. In a saucepan, combine all ingredients over medium heat.
2. Bring to a boil and cook up to thickened, about 40 to 45 mins.

3. To avoid sticking, stir often.
4. Allow it cool, then pour into a jar and refrigerate for up to two weeks.

Nutrition (per 2 tbsp):

Cals: 50, Carbs: 13g

Sugars: 9g, Fiber: 1g

Fat: 0g Protein: 0.2g

35.GREEN TOMATO CHUTNEY

Prep Time: 20 mins

Cook Time: 1 hr

Total Time: 1 hr 20 mins

Servings: 3 cups of

Ingredients:

- 4 cups of chop-up green tomatoes
- 1 cup of chop-up onions
- 1 apple, peel off and chop-up
- ½ cup of raisins
- ¾ cup of brown sugar
- 1 cup of apple cider vinegar
- 1 tsp mustard seeds
- ½ tsp ground ginger
- ½ tsp ground cinnamon
- ¼ tsp ground cloves
- 1 tsp salt

Instructions:

1. In a big saucepan, combine all ingredients.
2. Bring to a boil, then lower the heat and simmer, stirring regularly, for one hr.
3. Allow to cool before transferring to jars once thickened and jammy.
4. You may keep it in the fridge for up to a month.

Nutrition (per 2 tbsp):

Cals: 45, Carbs: 11g

Sugars: 9g, Fiber: 1g

Fat: 0g, Protein: 0.3g

36.ONION BACON JAM

Prep Time: 10 mins

Cook Time: 45 mins

Total Time: 55 mins

Servings: 12 (about 1 tbsp every)

Ingredients:

- 1 lb bacon, chop-up
- 2 Big sweet onions, thinly split
- 1/4 cup of brown sugar
- 1/2 cup of brewed coffee
- 1/4 cup of apple cider vinegar
- 1 tbsp balsamic vinegar
- Salt and pepper as needed

Instructions:

1. In a skillet, cook bacon over medium heat up to crispy. Take out and put aside.
2. Sauté onions in bacon grease for 20 to 25 mins, or up to they are caramelized.
3. Add bacon, vinegars, coffee, and brown sugar and stir.
4. Simmer up to thickened, stirring regularly, on low for 20 mins.
5. Store in a container once cooled. Store in the refrigerator.

Nutrition (per tbsp):

Cals: 120, Fat: 9g

Carbs: 6g, Protein: 4g

37.ROASTED GARLIC SPREAD

Prep Time: 5 mins

Cook Time: 40 mins

Total Time: 45 mins

Ingredients:

- 2 heads garlic
- 1 tbsp olive oil
- Pinch of salt
- Non-compulsory: 1 tbsp cream cheese or butter for smoothness

Instructions:

1. Turn the oven on to 400°F, or 200°C.
2. Take out the tops of the garlic heads, then cover them in foil, sprinkle them with salt, and drizzle them with oil.
3. The cloves Must be tender and brown after 35 to 40 mins of roasting.
4. Put the garlic in a bowl, squeeze it out, and mash it. If using, stir with butter or cream cheese.
5. Refrigerate or serve warm.

Nutrition (per serving):

Cals: 45, Fat: 3.5g

Carbs: 3g, Protein: 1g

38.CLASSIC MARINARA SAUCE

Prep Time: 10 mins

Cook Time: 30 mins

Total Time: 40 mins

Servings: 6

Ingredients:

- 2 tbsp olive oil
- 1 mini onion, lightly chop-up
- 3 cloves garlic, chop-up
- 1 (28 oz) can crushed tomatoes
- 1 tsp dried oregano
- 1/2 tsp sugar
- Salt and pepper as needed
- Fresh basil (non-compulsory)

Instructions:

1. In a saucepan, heat the olive oil. Cook the onions up to they are tender.
2. Add the garlic and heat for one min.
3. Add the sugar, salt, pepper, tomatoes, and oregano.
4. Simmer for half an hr without cover. If desired, add basil toward the end.
5. Leave lumpy or blend for a smoother texture.

Nutrition (per serving):

Cals: 90, Fat: 5g

Carbs: 9g

Protein: 2g

39.ROASTED TOMATO SALSA

Prep Time: 10 mins

Cook Time: 20 mins

Total Time: 30 mins

Servings: 8

Ingredients:

- 4 Big tomatoes, halved
- 1 mini onion, quartered
- 2 garlic cloves, peel off
- 1 jalapeño, halved
- 1 tbsp olive oil
- Juice of 1 lime
- 1/4 cup of cilantro
- Salt as needed

Instructions:

1. Set the oven temperature to 425°F (220°C).
2. Arrange the jalapeño, tomatoes, onion, and garlic on a baking sheet and brush with olive oil.
3. Roast up to charred, about 20 mins.
4. Once somewhat cooled, combine with salt, cilantro, and lime juice up to the desired consistency is achieved.

5. Serve cold or at room temperature.

Nutrition (per serving):

Cals: 35, Fat: 2g, Carbs: 4g

Protein: 1g

40.PEVERY SALSA

Prep Time: 15 mins

Cook Time: 0 mins

Total Time: 15 mins

Servings: 6

Ingredients:

- 3 ripe peveryes, diced
- 1/2 red bell pepper, diced
- 1/2 red onion, lightly chop-up
- 1 mini jalapeño, chop-up
- Juice of 1 lime
- 1/4 cup of chop-up cilantro
- Salt as needed

Instructions:

1. Put the bell pepper, onion, cilantro, jalapeño, and peveryes in a bowl.
2. Add salt and lime juice. Stir well.
3. Before serving, let it cool for at least half an hr.

Nutrition (per serving):

Cals: 40, Fat: 0g

Carbs: 10g, Protein: 1g

41.CORN AND BLACK BEAN SALSA

Prep Time: 15 mins

Cook Time: 0 mins

Total Time: 15 mins

Servings: 6

Ingredients:

- 1 can (15 oz) black beans, rinsed and drained
- 1 cup of corn kernels (fresh, canned, or thawed from refrigerate)
- 1 red bell pepper, diced
- 1 mini red onion, lightly chop-up
- 1 jalapeño, seeded and chop-up
- 1/4 cup of fresh cilantro, chop-up
- Juice of 2 limes
- 1 tbsp olive oil
- Salt and pepper as needed

Instructions:

1. Put the black beans, corn, onion, bell pepper, and jalapeño in a big bowl.
2. Add the olive oil, cilantro, and lime juice.
3. Add salt and pepper as needed and toss everything together.
4. For optimal taste, chill for half an hr or serve right away.

Nutrition (per serving):

Cals: 120 | Fat: 3g | Carbs: 19g | Protein: 5g | Fiber: 6g

42.SPICY TOMATILLO SALSA

Prep Time: 10 mins

Cook Time: 15 mins

Total Time: 25 mins

Servings: 6

Ingredients:

- 1 lb tomatillos, husked and rinsed
- 2 serrano chiles (or jalapeños for less heat), stemmed
- 2 garlic cloves
- 1/2 cup of chop-up white onion
- 1/4 cup of fresh cilantro

- Juice of 1 lime
- Salt as needed

Instructions:

1. Simmer the chiles and tomatillos in water for 10 to 12 mins, or up to they are tender. Empty.
2. Process the cilantro, garlic, onion, chiles, and tomatillos in a blender up to smooth.
3. As needed, add salt and lime juice.
4. Serve warm or chilled alongside grilled meats, tacos, or chips.

Nutrition (per serving):

Cals: 35 | Fat: 0.5g | Carbs: 7g | Protein: 1g | Fiber: 2g

43.APPLE BARBECUE SAUCE

Prep Time: 10 mins

Cook Time: 30 mins

Total Time: 40 mins

Servings: 8

Ingredients:

- 1 tbsp olive oil
- 1/2 onion, lightly chop-up
- 1 apple, peel off and finely grated
- 2 cloves garlic, chop-up
- 1 cup of ketchup
- 1/4 cup of apple cider vinegar
- 1/4 cup of brown sugar
- 1 tbsp Dijon mustard
- 1 tsp smoked paprika
- Salt and pepper as needed

Instructions:

1. In a saucepan, heat the olive oil. Cook the onion up to it becomes tender.
2. Sauté the apple and garlic for two to three mins.
3. Add the remaining ingredients and stir. Bring to a simmer.
4. Cook up to thickened, uncovered, 20 to 25 mins.

5. If you want a smooth texture, blend.

Nutrition (per serving):

Cals: 80 | Fat: 2g | Carbs: 16g | Protein: 1g | Sugar: 12g

44.CRANBERRY KETCHUP

Prep Time: 5 mins

Cook Time: 20 mins

Total Time: 25 mins

Servings: 8

Ingredients:

- 1 cup of fresh or refrigerate cranberries
- 1/2 cup of ketchup
- 1/4 cup of apple cider vinegar
- 1/4 cup of brown sugar
- 1/2 tsp ground cinnamon
- 1/4 tsp ground cloves
- Salt as needed

Instructions:

1. In a saucepan, combine all the ingredients.
2. Bring to a boil, then simmer up to the sauce thickens and the cranberries pop, 15 to 20 mins.
3. Blend up to it's smooth. Before serving, let it cool.

Nutrition (per serving):

Cals: 60 | Fat: 0g | Carbs: 15g | Sugar: 12g | Fiber: 1g

45. CHILI GARLIC SAUCE

Prep Time: 10 mins

Cook Time: 5 mins

Total Time: 15 mins

Servings: 12

Ingredients:

- 1 cup of red chilies, chop-up (fresno or Thai)
- 6 cloves garlic, peel off
- 1/4 cup of white vinegar
- 2 tbsp sugar
- 1 tsp salt
- 2 tbsp neutral oil

Instructions:

1. Make a coarse paste with the chiles, garlic, vinegar, sugar, and salt.
2. In a skillet, heat the oil, add the paste, and stir up to aromatic, 3 to 5 mins.
3. Chill and keep in the refrigerator in a jar.

Nutrition (per serving):

Cals: 25 | Fat: 1.5g | Carbs: 3g | Sugar: 2g | Fiber: 0.5g

46.BLUEBERRY SYRUP

Prep Time: 5 mins

Cook Time: 20 mins

Total Time: 25 mins

Servings: 12 (1 tbsp every)

Ingredients:

- 2 cups of fresh or refrigerate blueberries
- 1 cup of water
- 3/4 cup of sugar
- 1 tsp lemon juice
- 1/2 tsp vanilla extract (non-compulsory)

Instructions:

1. Put the blueberries, water, and sugar in a saucepan. Bring to a boil.
2. Reduce the heat and simmer for 15 mins, periodically mashing the berries.
3. Press on the solids while you strain the Mixture through a fine-mesh sieve.
4. Add vanilla essence and lemon juice and stir.
5. Allow to cool and keep in the refrigerator for up to two weeks in a sterile container.

Nutrition (per tbsp):

Cals: 45, Carbs: 12g

Sugars: 11g, Fat: 0g

Protein: 0g

47. STRAWBERRY RHUBARB SYRUP

Prep Time: 10 mins

Cook Time: 25 mins

Total Time: 35 mins

Servings: 12 (1 tbsp every)

Ingredients:

- 1 cup of diced rhubarb
- 1 cup of chop-up strawberries
- 1 cup of water
- 3/4 cup of sugar
- 1 tsp lemon zest (non-compulsory)

Instructions:

1. Put the rhubarb, strawberries, water, and sugar in a saucepan.
2. Heat till boiling, then lower the heat to a simmer and stew for 20 mins.
3. Use a strainer with fine mesh.
4. Add lemon zest and allow to cool.
5. Keep in the refrigerator for up to two weeks.

Nutrition (per tbsp):

Cals: 40, Carbs: 11g

Sugars: 10g, Fat: 0g

Protein: 0g

48. VANILLA PEAR SYRUP

Prep Time: 10 mins

Cook Time: 20 mins

Total Time: 30 mins

Servings: 12 (1 tbsp every)

Ingredients:

- 2 ripe pears, peel off and chop-up
- 1 cup of water
- 3/4 cup of sugar
- 1/2 tsp vanilla extract
- 1 tsp lemon juice

Instructions:

1. In a saucepan, combine sugar, water, and diced pears.
2. Pears Must be tender after 20 mins of simmering over medium heat.
3. Blend and strain the blend.
4. Add lemon juice and vanilla and stir.
5. Before putting away in a jar, let it cool.

Nutrition (per tbsp):

Cals: 42, Carbs: 11g

Sugars: 10g, Fat: 0g

Protein: 0g

49. ELDERFLOWER CORDIAL

Prep Time: 15 mins

Cook Time: 10 mins

Total Time: 25 mins + 24 hrs steeping

Servings: 24 (1 tbsp every)

Ingredients:

- 20 elderflower heads (fresh, not sprayed)
- 4 cups of water
- 4 cups of sugar
- 1 lemon, split

- 1 tbsp citric acid

Instructions:

1. Bring the sugar and water to a boil, then turn off the heat.
2. Add lemon slices, citric acid, and elderflowers and stir.
3. Cover and steep for 24 hrs at room temperature.
4. Strain through fine mesh or cheesecloth.
5. For up to a month, bottle and store in the refrigerator.

Nutrition (per tbsp):

Cals: 50, Carbs: 13g

Sugars: 12g, Fat: 0g

Protein: 0g

50. CHERRY LIME CORDIAL

Prep Time: 10 mins

Cook Time: 20 mins

Total Time: 30 mins

Servings: 16 (1 tbsp every)

Ingredients:

- 2 cups of pitted cherries (fresh or refrigerate)
- 1 cup of water
- 1 cup of sugar
- Juice of 2 limes
- Zest of 1 lime

Instructions:

1. For 20 mins, simmer the cherries, water, and sugar over medium heat.
2. Take off the heat and combine in the zest and lime juice.
3. Press down to take out the liquid as you strain through a sieve.
4. Cool and store in the refrigerator for up to two weeks.

Nutrition (per tbsp):

Cals: 45, Carbs: 11g

Sugars: 10g, Fat: 0g

Protein: 0g

51.CLASSIC SAUERKRAUT

Prep Time: 20 mins
Fermentation Time: 1–4 weeks
Total Time: 1 week minimum
Servings: 20 (1 tbsp per serving)

Ingredients:

- 1 medium green cabbage (about 2–3 lbs)
- 1–1.5 tbsp sea salt (non-iodized)
- Non-compulsory: 1 tsp caraway seeds (for flavor)

Instructions:

1. To prepare the cabbage, slice off the outer leaves and core, then shred it lightly.
2. Put the cabbage in a big basin and massage it with salt. Season with salt. For five to ten mins, massage the cabbage till the liquid is out.
3. Pack into Jar: Fill a clean jar with cabbage and its liquid, leaving a 1-inch headspace. Use a clean little jar or a fermentation weight to weigh it down.
4. Ferment: Cover with a cloth or breathable cover. For one to four weeks, keep at room temperature (60 to 75°F).
5. Verify Every day: Check for bubbles and press down on any floating cabbage. After seven days, taste and keep fermenting up to the desired tanginess is achieved.
6. Store: For up to six months after fermentation, seal and place in the refrigerator.

Nutrition (per serving):

Cals: 5, Carbs: 1g

Fiber: 0.5g, Sodium: 150mg

Vitamin C: 10% DV

52. FERMENTED GARLIC HONEY

Prep Time: 10 mins
Fermentation Time: 1 month

Total Time: 1 month
Servings: 40 (1 tsp per serving)

Ingredients:

- 1 cup of raw, peel off garlic cloves
- 1 cup of raw honey (local preferred)

Instructions:

1. Jar Garlic and Honey: Fill a clean jar with peel off garlic. Cover with honey up to completely coated.
2. Ferment: Use a fermentation lid or loosely cap. Keep out of direct sunlight and store at room temperature.
3. Stir Daily: To coat the garlic, flip or gently stir every day for the first week.
4. Bubble Watch: In three to five days, fermentation will start. Give it a minimum of one month to sit.
5. Store: After the flavor intensifies, cover the jar and store it in the refrigerator or a cold pantry.

Nutrition (per serving):

Cals: 22, Carbs: 6g

Sugar: 5g

53. SPICY KIMCHI

Prep Time: 40 mins
Fermentation Time: 3–14 days
Total Time: 3+ days
Servings: 20

Ingredients:

- 1 medium Napa cabbage
- 1/4 cup of sea salt (non-iodized)
- Water (filtered)
- 1 tbsp finely grated ginger
- 1 tbsp chop-up garlic
- 1 tbsp sugar
- 2 tbsp fish sauce (or soy sauce for vegan)
- 2–4 tbsp Korean red pepper flakes (gochugaru)

- 4 green onions, split
- 1 medium carrot, julienned
- 1 mini daikon radish, julienned

Instructions:

1. Chop the cabbage and let it soak for two hrs in salted water. Drain well and rinse.
2. To make the paste, combine the gochugaru, fish sauce, sugar, ginger, and garlic.
3. Combine the vegetables: Add the green onions, radish, cabbage, carrots, and spice paste. Put on some gloves!
4. Pack and Ferment: Press down to release liquid after packing snugly into the jar. Give yourself one inch of headroom.
5. Ferment: Leave it covered for three to five days at room temperature. Taste every day.
6. Store in the refrigerator for up to six months when it's sour enough as needed.

Nutrition (per serving):

Cals: 15, Carbs: 3g

Fiber: 1g, Vitamin A: 15% DV

Probiotics: High

54. LACTO-FERMENTED CARROTS

Prep Time: 15 mins
Fermentation Time: 5–10 days
Total Time: ~1 week
Servings: 15

Ingredients:

- 4 Big carrots, peel off and slice into sticks
- 2 cups of water (filtered)
- 1 tbsp sea salt (non-iodized)
- 1 clove garlic (non-compulsory)
- 1/2 tsp mustard seeds or dill (non-compulsory)

Instructions:

1. Dissolve salt with water to make brine.
2. Jar of Packs: In a clean container, arrange the carrots upright. If using, add the spices or garlic.
3. Add Brine: Cover the carrots with brine, allowing a 1-inch headspace.
4. Weigh and Cover: To keep carrots immersed, use a weight. Cover loosely.
5. Ferment: Give it five to ten days at room temperature. After five days, taste.
6. Once tangy, store in the refrigerator for up to two months.

Nutrition (per serving):

Cals: 10, Carbs: 2g

Fiber: 0.5g

Vitamin A: 50% DV

Probiotics: Present

55. DILL FERMENTED CUCUMBERS (PICKLES)

Prep Time: 15 mins
Fermentation Time: 5–7 days
Total Time: ~1 week
Servings: 15

Ingredients:

- 6 mini pickling cucumbers
- 2 cups of filtered water
- 1 tbsp sea salt
- 2–3 garlic cloves
- 2–3 sprigs fresh dill
- 1/2 tsp mustard seeds (non-compulsory)
- Grape leaf or bay leaf (non-compulsory, helps with crunch)

Instructions:

1. Make a brine by dissolving salt in water.
2. Fill the jar with the spices, garlic, dill, and cucumbers.
3. Pour the brine over the cucumbers up to they are completely immersed.
4. Add weight after weighing and covering. Use a towel or a loose lid to cover.
5. Ferment: Leave for 5–7 days at ambient temperature (65–75°F). If tightly covered, burp every day.
6. Once tangy, store in the refrigerator for up to two months.

Nutrition (per serving):

Cals: 5, Carbs: 1g

Sodium: 150mg

Fiber: 0.3g, Probiotics: Rich source

56. BLACK BEAN AND CORN QUESADILLAS

Prep Time: 10 mins

Cook Time: 10 mins

Total Time: 20 mins

Servings: 4

Ingredients:

- 1 tbsp olive oil
- 1 can black beans, drained and rinsed
- 1 cup of corn kernels (fresh or refrigerate)
- 1 tsp cumin
- 1 tsp chili powder
- Salt and pepper as needed
- 8 flour tortillas
- 1 1/2 cups of shredded cheddar cheese
- 1 tbsp chop-up cilantro (non-compulsory)
- Sour cream for serving (non-compulsory)

Instructions:

1. In a pan, heat the olive oil over medium heat. Add corn, black beans, chili powder, cumin, salt, and pepper. Cook up to well heated, about 5 mins.
2. Use a microwave or a dry skillet to reheat tortillas.
3. Put the quesadillas together: Cover half of every tortilla with the bean and corn Mixture, and then top with cheese.
4. Cook the tortillas in the pan over medium heat for two to three mins on every side, or up to golden and crispy, after folding them in half.
5. If desired, top with sour cream and cilantro after sliceting into wedges.

Nutrition (per serving):

Cals: 400, Protein: 15g

Carbs: 50g, Fat: 15g

Fiber: 10g

57. SWEET POTATO AND LENTIL STEW

Prep Time: 15 mins

Cook Time: 30 mins

Total Time: 45 mins

Servings: 4

Ingredients:

- 1 tbsp olive oil
- 1 onion, chop-up
- 2 cloves garlic, chop-up
- 2 medium sweet potatoes, peel off and cubed
- 1 cup of dried lentils, rinsed
- 1 can diced tomatoes
- 1 tsp turmeric
- 1 tsp cumin
- 4 cups of vegetable broth
- Salt and pepper as needed
- Fresh parsley for garnish

Instructions:

1. In a Big saucepan, heat the olive oil over medium heat. Sauté the garlic and onion for around five mins, or up to they are tender.
2. Add the lentils, sweet potatoes, cumin, turmeric, chop-up tomatoes, vegetable broth, salt, and pepper. Combine to blend.
3. After bringing to a boil, lower the heat and simmer for half an hr, or up to the sweet potatoes and lentils are soft.
4. Serve after adding some fresh parsley as a garnish.

Nutrition (per serving):

Cals: 350, Protein: 18g

58.BAKED POTATO WITH SOUR CREAM AND BACON

Prep Time: 10 mins

Cook Time: 1 hr

Total Time: 1 hr 10 mins

Servings: 4

Ingredients:

- 4 Big russet potatoes
- 4 strips of bacon
- 1 cup of sour cream
- 1/2 cup of shredded cheddar cheese
- 1/4 cup of chop-up green onions
- Salt and pepper as needed

Instructions:

1. Set the oven's temperature to 400°F, or 200°C.
2. After cleaning and washing the potatoes, use a fork to make a few holes in them.
3. After placing the potatoes directly on the oven rack, bake them for 45 to 1 hr, or up to they are soft.
4. In a skillet, fry the bacon over medium heat up to it crisps up. Take off the heat and crush it.
5. After cooking, slice potatoes open and use a fork to fluff the insides.
6. Add green onions, bacon crumbles, shredded cheddar cheese, and sour cream on top of every potato. Add salt and pepper for seasoning.

Nutrition (per serving):

Cals: 380, Protein: 9g

Carbs: 45g, Fat: 18g

Fiber: 5g, Sodium: 750mg

Made in the USA
Columbia, SC
23 May 2025

58364872R00028